TED CRUZ is RUNNING for PRESIDENT!

A 2016 Presidential Election Coloring Book

ISBN 9781514784419
Cover by Smerdloff

Ted Cruz wants to be America's next President...

...and live in the White House.

Ted lives in Texas,
with his wife
and their two daughters.

Ted was born on
December 22, 1970,
in Calgary, Alberta, Canada.

He grew up in Texas.

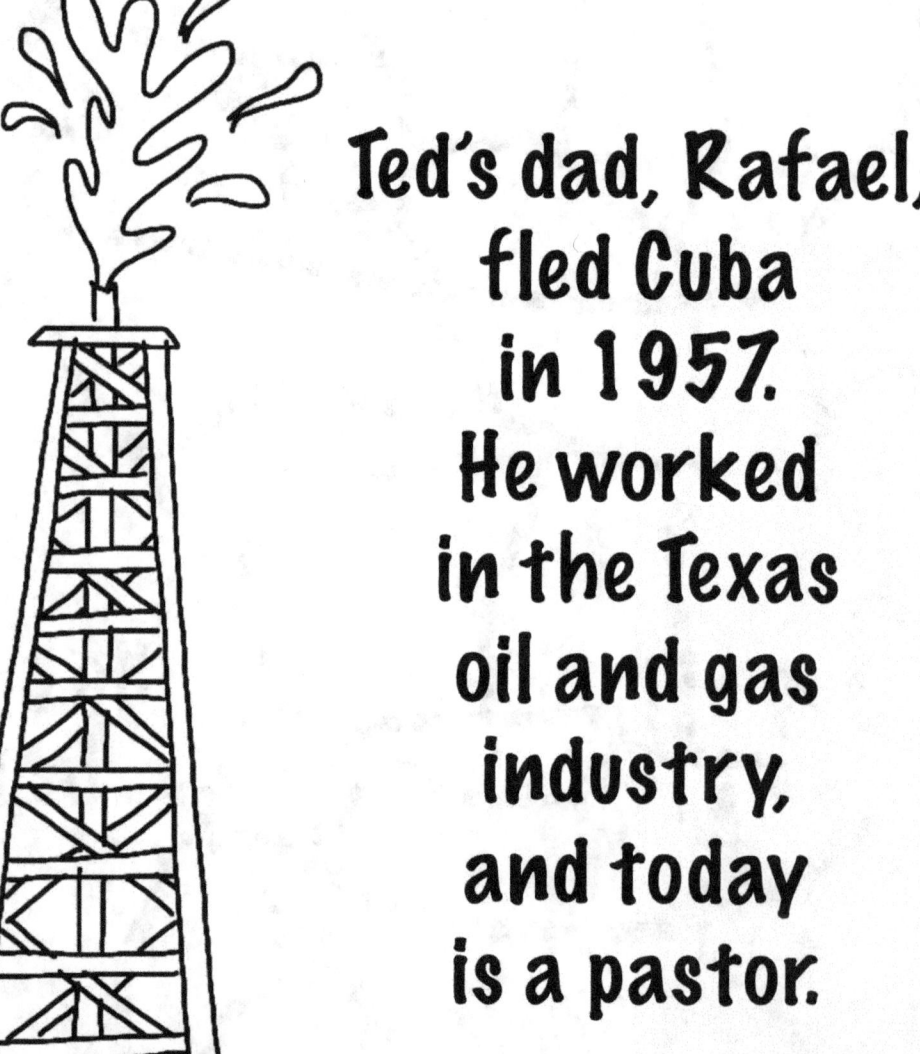

Ted's dad, Rafael, fled Cuba in 1957. He worked in the Texas oil and gas industry, and today is a pastor.

Ted's mom, Eleanor,
was a
computer programmer.

We
the People

United States, in Order to form a more perfect Un

, insure domestic Tranquility, provide for the cor

ral Welfare, and secure the Blessings of Liberty t

ordain and establish this Constitution for the Un

Section. 1. All legislative Powers herein granted

United States, which shall consist of a Senate a

2. The House of Representatives shall be con

Year by the People of the several States, a

alifications requisite for Electors of the

No Person shall be a Represen

five Years, and been seven

en elected, be an Inha

direct Taxes sho

in this Un

At 13, Ted joined an after-school program where he memorized the U.S. Constitution, read and discussed conservative economists such as Hayek and Friedman, and spoke to audiences across Texas.

Ted was a champion debater in college (at Princeton) and in law school (at Harvard), and he won National Speaker of the Year in 1992.

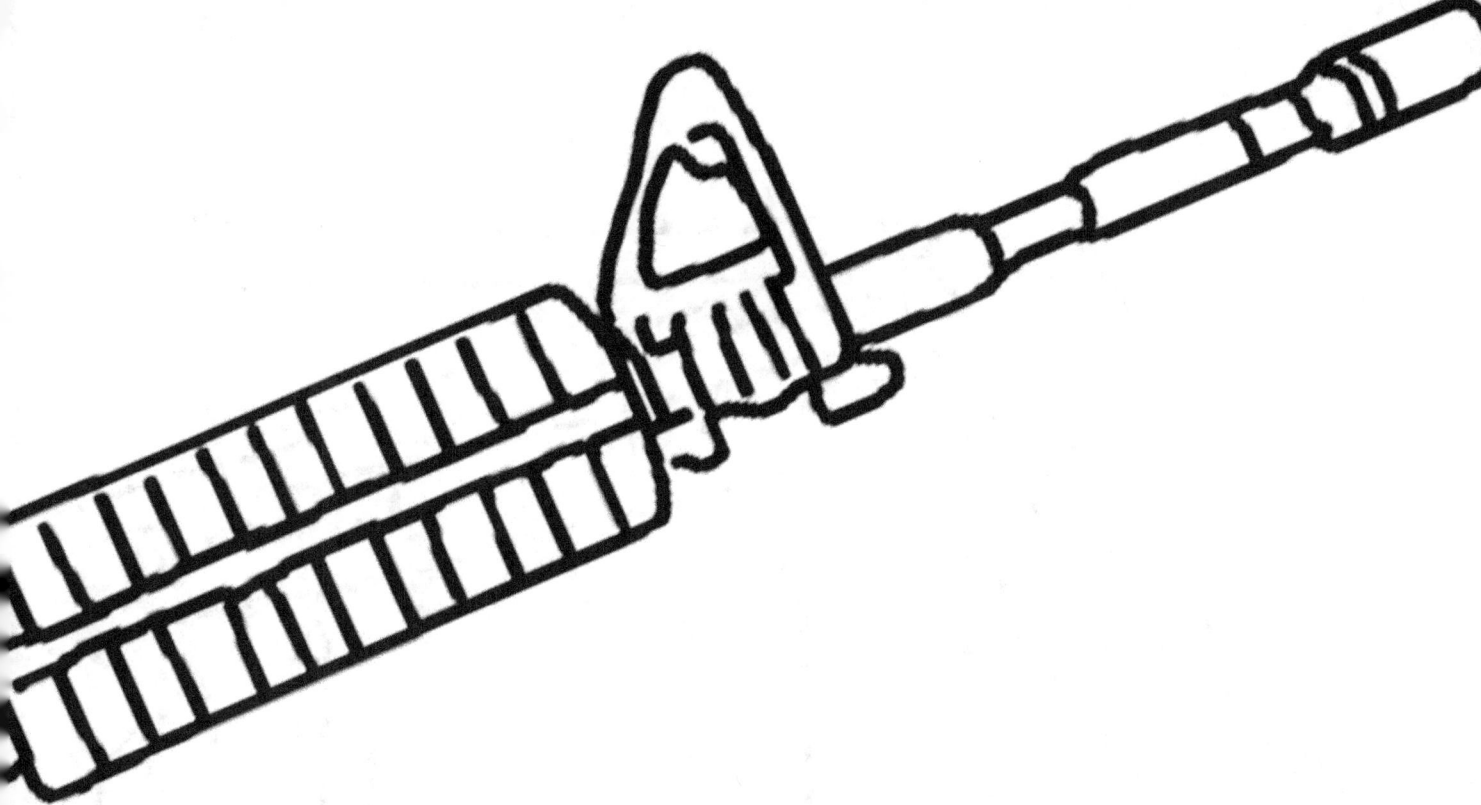

As a young lawyer, Ted represented the National Rifle Association. He was legal counsel to the George W. Bush campaign in 1999 and 2000, and played an important role in the Florida recount case.

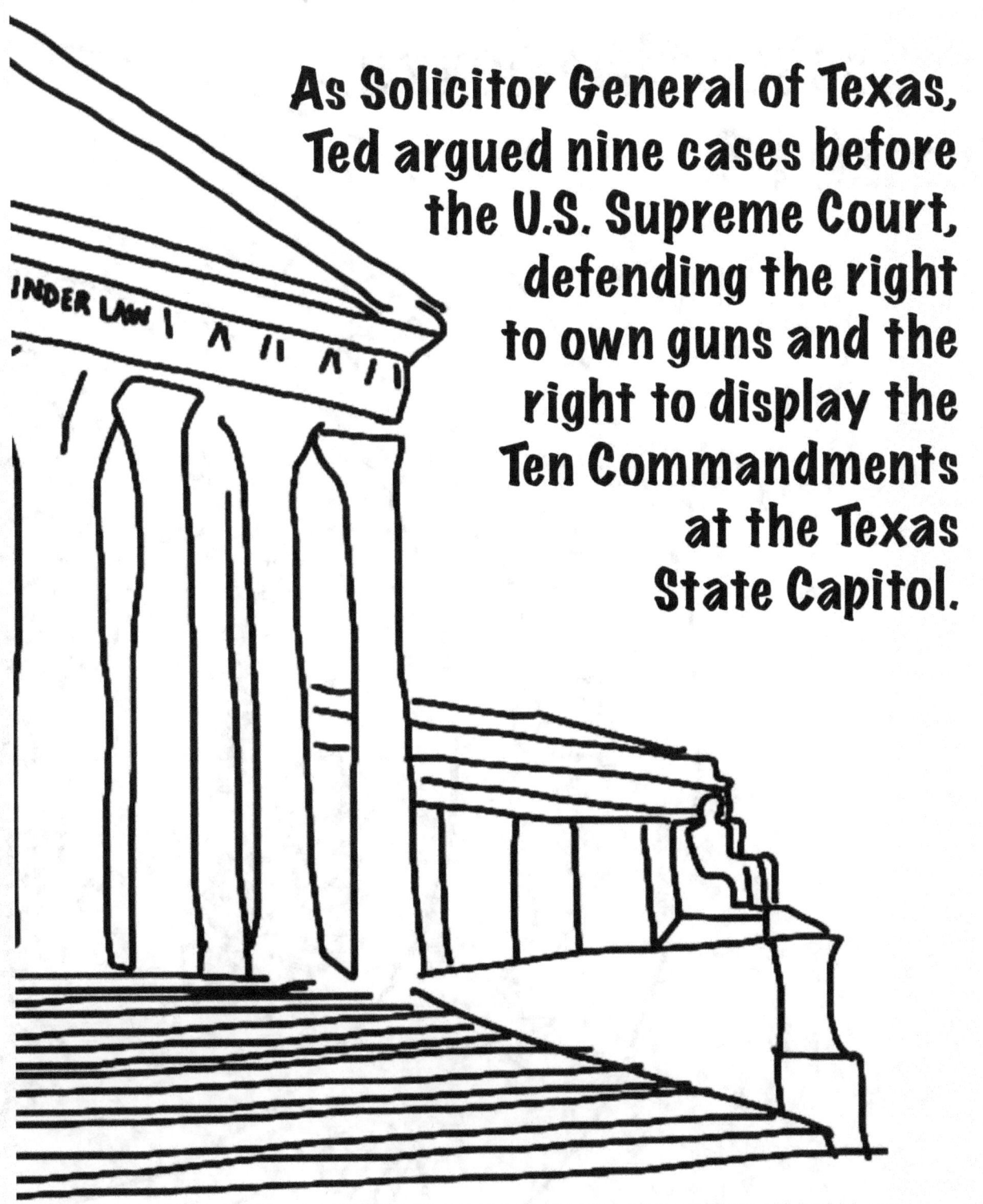

As Solicitor General of Texas, Ted argued nine cases before the U.S. Supreme Court, defending the right to own guns and the right to display the Ten Commandments at the Texas State Capitol.

Ted became a U.S. Senator, representing Texas, in 2013.

T A T E S ★ ★

Cracker Jack
BALL PLAYERS

JOHNSON, WASHINGTON-AMERICANS

The President oversees the Internal Revenue Service, which collects our taxes to pay for government services.

Ted believes the IRS should be abolished, and replaced with a simple "flat tax" for every American.

On immigration, Ted Cruz favors reforms that emphasize the Rule of Law.

"Instead of the lawlessness and the president's unconstitutional executive amnesty, imagine a president that finally, finally, finally secures the borders," he said.

Ted favors a dramatic expansion of school choice vouchers, and opposes the Common Core standards.

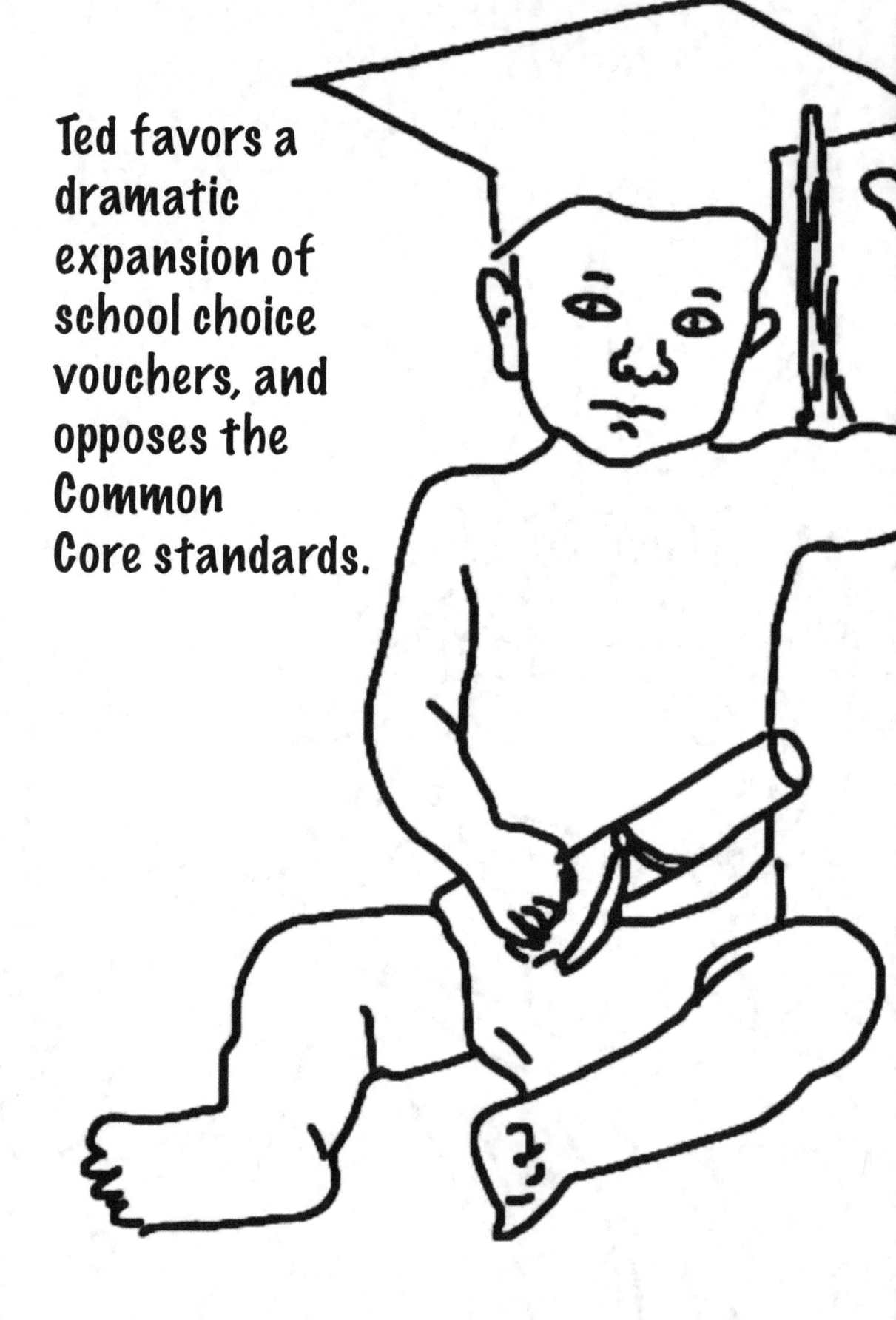

"As a first principle for education reform, Congress should advance school choice for America's children," he said.

Ted Cruz loves America,

and wants to make
Our country better.

November 8th, 2016, is Election Day.

Will America choose **Ted Cruz?**

Draw yourself as President!

www.ingramcontent.com/pod-product-compliance
Lightning Source LLC
Chambersburg PA
CBHW080936290526

45795CB00007BA/2773